asking myself
answering myself

WITHDRAWN

No longer the property of the
Boston Public Library.
Sale of this material benefits the Library.

D1027237

asking myself
answering myself

By

SHIMPEI KUSANO

Translated by Cid Corman, with Susumu Kamaike

A NEW DIRECTIONS BOOK

Copyright © 1969, 1978, 1980, 1984 by Cid Corman

All rights reserved. Except for brief passages quoted in a newspaper, maga-
zine, radio, or television review, no part of this book may be reproduced in
any form or by any means, electronic or mechanical, including photocopying
and recording, or by any information storage and retrieval system, without
permission in writing from the Publisher.

Sections of this book were first published in *frogs & others,* poems by
Shimpei Kusano, designed and produced by Mushinsha Limited, Tokyo,
1969. Other parts first appeared in *Origin,* fourth series, nos. 5 and 13. Grate-
ful acknowledgment is made to both Mushinsha and *Origin.*

Manufactured in the United States of America
First published as New Directions Paperbook 556 in 1984
Published simultaneously in Canada by George J. MacLeod, Ltd., Toronto

Library of Congress Cataloging in Publication Data

Kusano, Shinpei, 1903–
    Asking myself/answering myself.
    (A New Directions Book)
    1. Kusano, Shimpei, 1903–   —Translations, English.
I. Corman, Cid.   II. Kamaike, Susumu.   III. Title
PL832.U75A23   1984   895.6'14   83-17481
ISBN 0–8112–0887–7

New Directions Books are published for James Laughlin
by New Directions Publishing Corporation
80 Eighth Avenue, New York 10011

TABLE OF CONTENTS

INTRODUCTION

The Orient, principally India, China, and Japan, has managed somehow through the hard-won intelligence (art) of a few tough souls to come to a sense of scale—that makes sense, that casts man into his minimality in the face of the geography of time. This has in no way eliminated—even under the title of Enlightenment—the existential ache, though it may provide momentary lapses.

Shimpei Kusano's frogs, familiar as they are at once, are utterly Oriental configurations. They are the voices of proportion, muting wisdom even as they suffer it. They are the voices of nature—in its largest sense—and of absolute innocence. They sing in the face of every moment's doom. They live beyond any idea of PROGRESS. They are the gaiety and spontaneity and love and rootedness of fear in man. They mock our pretensions, but share them too—gently. They are a society whose limits are prehistoric and posthistoric. They live beyond abuse within the nature of man's spirit.

There are more than (or less than, if you will) frogs in Kusano's world, naturally. But the city, the landscapes, the denizens, all find their point of reference in these small leapers in their inland swamps and pools and rivers. Is it only (!) imagination that makes one seem small beside them? And is it only imagination that makes the Aristophanic croakings their chronicler indites as sweet in their provocation as any of our too often less perceived utterances?

Kusano-san is a poet for whom it is hard to find a parallel, either today or in the past. His poetry is like a sort of modern folklore. There isn't a child in Japan who isn't familiar with some of his frog poems. And of course no adult.

In addition, he is so well-known a personality that he is a frequent talk show visitor on Japanese T.V. The royal family turns to him for occasional poetry, making him almost the nation's poet laureate. At the same time, he is well-known for his sympathies with the working class (he was an early translator of Carl Sandburg and prides himself on having met Sun Yat-sen as well as Tagore).

Kusano was born in Nagano, Japan in 1903, and he learned his idiosyncratic English in Canton over fifty years ago. All together, he has spent eleven years in China—longer than any other modern Japanese poet—and this relation to China touches his language deeply. He often draws upon Chinese words that won't be found in Japanese dictionaries. And that—along with other special turns—makes some of his poems very difficult to translate.

One of the problems in translating modern Japanese (especially Japanese poetry) is the general use of several ways of *writing* words within a single poem. For example, the Japanese poet can transliterate certain words in various ways. In Kusano's poem "Asking Myself/Answering Myself," the repeated nonwords are identical sounds throughout but written in various ways.

Why is this done? A word written in *kanji* (Chinese ideogrammic form) has a more formal literary cast. A word written in *katakana* (reductive syllabic forms that have only sound value on the face of it) is always foreign or for public display, and seems "easier" and more modern. *Hiragana* is the same reduction, but written in a more cursive and thus colloquial way. On top of all this (and you must realize that the Japanese written language—let alone spoken—has probably undergone more changes in this century than any other language), words are often used in foreign—Roman—spelling also. This is especially true of English words. And how do you translate an English word into English? You may think it simpler to just leave it be, but often the word has a different meaning from that to which we are accustomed, and the tone is almost invariably different. As a result, one is tempted to use the English word in quotes and add a footnote to explain it!

Kusano's verses often break into song or into plain text. They are always punctuated by periods, occasionally by parentheses, and more rarely by commas and exclamation marks. Refrains, or musical passages, are generally free of punctuation.

Because Japanese, of course, has no recourse to capitalization and because the poet's syntactic economy does not always fall back upon sentence structure, we have dispensed with capitals at the start of lines of sentences. Proper names, however, have been marked whenever clarity is at stake.

Sometimes the poet's words are so precisely Japanese in reference and character—in the use of specific nouns mostly—that dictionary meanings, even when scientifically accurate, become hopeless. Certain foods or flowers are stubbornly indigenous and take on overtones that translation cares enough not to reduce. By and large we feel that contexts make such nuances reasonably apparent or suggest them.

It cannot be too strongly urged upon the reader that seemingly nonsense-syllable sound effects are vital components—many sounding after the "sense" of the poems has gone *into* sense. The poems, in any event, are meant to be enjoyed in the voicing—without exception. But don't shut your eyes either.

A note on pronunciation: in the Japanese words, names, and sounds, each syllable merits equal stress, unless otherwise indicated. Consonants have been doubled at places to increase weight. Slurrings and stresses have also been marked, usually by '. Vowels are invariable and single in their sound-attachments: "a" sounds like "ah," "e" like our "hey," "i" as in "machine," "o" as in "or," and "u" as in "rule." Certain consonants are not quite the same as in English. What looks like 'l' is a trill, more nearly, on tongue and palate (*not* teeth). The "k" and "g" are hard sounds, but not harsh, and slightly aspirated. Exclamation marks are pronounced with the mouth wide open and no sound being uttered.

The last poem in this volume was written in 1983, and all together, the book spans fifty years of work. Painfully of our time, Shimpei Kusano's poetry sounds perspectives we have long forgotten, or never remembered are central to what we are and always must be: human beings. Feeling knows. As the man who made the poems that follow knows.

Cid Corman

BIRTHDAY PARTY

between sandbanks marsh reflecting twilight clouds.
purple mist rising.
the golden moondish risen.

bulrush and sedge marshedge.
on stalk leaf tip velvet pile of fireflies.
firefly light quick quick off/on.
on waterbeetle back waterspider. on catfish whiskers
        glimmering duckweed.

then.
equisetum flute fluted all around.
and all at once the marsh face full of frog faces.
making many circles solemnly quietly.
fireflies all together turn out their lights.
all around the darkness springs up.
equisetum flute flutes again shrill all around.
Jubilee for the End of the Endless Serene 10,000 Years' Choir
        bulrush booming swaying all over.

      that's Gobila stood up maybe.
      or Glimma or Qayloqay maybe.
      in flickerings the choir ends.
      unusually tall zebra grass pressing against.
      after chanting deep bara-a-ra-bara-a.

          all our births'.
          all our joys'.
          one night of the year tonight.
          all our hearts beating.
          all our eyes flashing.
          celebrating all our futures.
          all of us. . . .

drink and sing. buddies—jabojabojabo—jabo light's
      whirlpool.

killifish glitteringly splash.
innumerable fireflies streaming mingle.

li- li- lililu lililu liffuffuffuff'
li- li- lililu lililu liffuffuffuff'

        lilinf fkenk'
        fkenk' kekekke
kekukku kekukku kensalili-olu
kekukku kekukku kensalili-olu
        biida-lala biida-lala
        binbin begank'
        biida-lala biida-lala
        binbin begank'
begank' begank' gaggaga-lili-ki
begank' begank' gaggaga-lili-ki
        galili-ki kikukku gaggaga-lili-ki
        galili-ki kikukku kukkuku gugugu
kikukku kukukku kukkuku gugugu
        gugugu gugunk'
        gugugugu gugunk'
gululut gululut iiiiiiiiiiiiiiiii
gululut gululut iiiiiiiiiiiiiiiii
        gamb'yan gamb'yan
          our dream.
          color of dawn.
          our song.
        gamb'yan gamb'yan

gyawalot'gyawalot'gyawa-lololololi(t)
gyawalot'gyawalot'gyawa-lololololi(t)
gyawalot'gyawalot'gyawa-lololololi(t)
gyawalot'gyawalot'gyawa-lololololi(t)
gyawalot'gyawalot'gyawa-lololololi(t)

gyawalot'gyawalot'gyawa-lololololi(t)
gyawalot'gyawalot'gyawa-lololololi(t)
gyawalot'gyawalot'gyawa-lololololi(t)

gyawalot'gyawalot'gyawa-lololololi(t)
gyawalot'gyawalot'gyawa-lololololi(t)
gyawalot'gyawalot'gyawa-lololololi(t)
gyawalot'gyawalot'gyawa-lololololi(t)

epilogue

as author I have no desire to stop the choir at this party celebrating birth. on the banks of O-Aza Kamiogawa in the village of Kamiogawa in the district of Iwaki in the prefecture of Fukushima. a party of points tinier than sesame seed as yet. this ecstasy's swaying echoing flowing place. but actually snow sifting outside, me in my poor *kotatsu*,* sitting crosslegged in heavy dark. meditation ending with what was born. (in my body some of the singing staying. now far faint ripples.) O already the strung lights of the fireflies have all gone out. a tangle of torn goldfish-weed only catching vainly at the big full moon.

---

* *Kotatsu:* a quilt over a table over some heating device. If one's feet are warm, one is warm, the Japanese believe.

"TEN THOUSAND YEARS, GOODBYE!"

in dark.
a great glass tower stands and.

a spiral glass tower stands and.
atop it as if on the verge of vertigo.
a frog.
up on one foot.
gazing at the far side of the universe.

      (o reader join him at that height)

now in the heavens dawn draws near.
eastward sad Nile blue.
ah "Ten Thousand Years, Goodbye!"
musical tadpoles all in staves.
quiet.
quiet.
move.

quiet.
quiet.
moving.

A WHILE

gee. like trachoma.
what a lovely moon.

somewhere hereabouts fox is munching something eh.
zebra grass grows wild there. when Qayloqay was little he
         got lost there you know.
no. whatever happened.
somehow he's still alive.
but.
but? every day at the brink alive somehow. nothing serious.
my but what a lovely moon huh.
oh.
that mountain what's behind it.
marshes mountains and ricefields. all the same.
beyond them?
more ricefields. fields. pear fields.
and beyond them?
way way beyond?
yes that's what I mean.
there's the sea. who was it. yuh. Qanimm.
they were boasting. the sea's a sky turned into a river.
then it must be also somehow blue huh.
even by day they say it's black. big & black alive.
good heavens!
the sand looks dazzling.

LULULU'S FUNERAL

(accompanied by Chopin's funeral march)

proceeding quietly single file.
long silent single file.
file of frogs proceeding.
on their brows blue fireflies set.
myriads of frogs proceeding.
pacing sand wastes of Japan.
pacing darkness of sand wastes.
quiet quietly proceeding.

        Lululu white.
        aflame.
        Lululu no longer.
        lovely Lululu no longer.
        shimmering petals.
        pour on Lululu.

        shimmering petals.
        pour on Lululu.

stream of ripples moving funeral.
singing quietly flowing.
in the dark wastes of Japan.
before it is known the singing too.
will have vanished away.
fireflies pale.
lights flickering vanishing.
in the inclining heavens.
crescent moon.

SHORT TUNE

snow falling on moon face.
full circle.
gray-dark splash-patterned snow falling.

on earth.
many many.
supposed-to-be-sleeping.
frogs' eyes.

some gaping.
gleaming.
frogs' eyes.

moon pallid.
paler than ghost.

       deeper.
       deeper.

nothing to see now.

ROCK

in rain wet by it.
by itself.
rock is.
is millions of years.
in vague.
mist.

DEATH

1.
out of a set of black teeth unconsciously.
an.
apparently white tooth emerges.
death is born.

death alone.

lamentation and consolation round about.
no longer concerns.
death.

down the linoleum corridor.
the rubberwheeled Fletcher wagon starts out.
accompanied by survivors.
quietly.

the thing on the sheet.
that's a corpse.
what knows the corpse.
is not death.
is corpse.

2.
the vertical cold tank.
(to the beat of a bell quicker than a metronome gone mad.)
oxygen.
fssss fssss.
in the field of night white mold quietly bursts.
as if another.
were born.

hesitant death.
hehho.
the universe gathering making small greetings hard to hear
            but man coming to know man's death comes after.

alone.
death.
not even a giggle.
death clutching the hands of death.

common yes.
the spirit of equality O.
death is alive.
death at length stands up.

3.
in the bustle of death.
I wash down. alcohol after a long interlude.
naturally down my throat.

death likely doesn't begrudge me sun but critical of my 60
         years.

death.
for the first time opens eyes.
and eyes open means eyes no longer open.

      (what's the rush.)

FALLING CHERRY BLOSSOMS

blossoms falling.
falling.
cherry cherry down down dancing down down dancing.

light and shadows mingle and.
more than snow.
more than death quietly cherry down dance.
down dance down down dancing.

light and dreams mingle and.
flickering gaslight shadows.
come forth and vanish.
blossoms falling.
falling.

in Oriental time.
creating dreams.
tossing them away.

blossoms falling.
falling.
blossoms falling fall.
cherry cherry down down dancing down down dancing.

MYSTERY OF WHITE & GREEN

of a pale snowy luster &.
pungency & sweetness.

under earth white swelling.
above earth green stretching.

(why do white & green divide)
(why do white & green unite)

this fresh mystery.

as far as.
as far as.
radish field.

NIGHT SEA

out of the distant ponderous depths.
out of the dark invisible endless past.

    zuzuzuzu wa'ru
    zuzuzun zuwa'ru
    gunun uwa'ru

the dark sea rumbling.
out of the blackness leaden waves are born and.
the splashing leaden mane of the waves dashed and.
crawls up on to the wet sands.
leaden waves are born out there and.
again out there are born and.
engulfed in India ink.
only to reappear and come on again.

    zuzuzuzu wa'ru
    zuzuzun zuwa'ru
    gunun uwa'ru

        likely it was at this midnight hour.
        mammoths trod.
        smelling like moldy rice-cake.
        all in a row.
        slithery sloppy.
        leaving huge rice-cake prints behind.
        after eating heartily.
        tromping off contentedly.
        into conspicuously darkest darkness out there.
        and heavily disappeared.

    zuzuzuzu wa'ru
    zuzuzun zuwa'ru
    gunun uwa'ru

over the boundless waste of Kujukuri Beach.
waves creeping in with leaden embroideries but.

licking the sands subside again into the blackest sea.
night without end rumbling.
returning to the vast.

    zuzuzuzu wa'ru
    zuzuzun zuwa'ru
    gunun uwa'ru

THE DESERT OF JAPAN

1.
blackest sea.
licking sand.
on a point of shale breaks.

2.
far away stretching.
ups and downs of dunes.

the far black.
pyramid Fuji.

3.
red.
one light burning.
a swerving panting train comes to a rattling halt.
suddenly coming out.
coming out coming out coming coming out.
certainly man men coming out.
coming out coming out cursing and laughing together
            coming coming.
coming out coming out brittle voices.
a pistol shot hustle and bustle scattering stir.
coming out coming out people very like men.
bustling about.
a whistle jets.
train starts.

4.
a bevy of angels.
like big moths flowing into sky.
a wheedling heartrending whistle and.
a wheedling heartrending whistle and.

lamentation bursts forth and.
some are lost in fog in turbulence flowing.
many moving off like snowy herons.
but more carefully seen men without stockings.

5.
poetry science philosophy standing near each other around a
            bonfire on the sand.
throbbing like a dynamo dreams course their entire bodies
            though the fire shivers and the flame is weak.
blue-red neon shines.
around that busy place there like a mirage.
likely Japanese culture.
pop songs etc. float forth.

6.
a clock strikes.
gan gon gan gon.
no building nothing seen but.
past midnight already.
gan gon gan gon.
won't stop going.

7.
like a hedgehog shedding light.
soon the great sun of morning will rise.
light will shine all around and.
the scent of the green element will also come full.
science will wander off into mountains and fields and towards
            precipices.
literature will go on probing probing to see human beings in
            full depth.
parks between air and air will be born and.
in the sea neon will bloom.
school a preparation.
society will be school.
politics will be the melting-pot of wisdom and devotion.

16

everyone will start to make a living.
inventions will produce inventions.
great philosophies will be born.
music will stir the aged.
medical science will be common sense.
cosmic rays will be more abundant and developed anew.
atomic energy will be made into fuel.
all cultures will move towards becoming classics.
duels will occur everywhere over beauty.
the unnecessary will be realized as unnecessary.
only beauty will vie with heaven and its eternity.

but these possibilities also.
if they just remain so.
will be retrograde.

8.
in worlds beyond the sea.
landings on open spaces of the moon and.
the great development of polar resources will also
              commence.

9.
the motionless sand's.
vast sea.

most crescent moon.

10.
ten millimeters the summit of Fuji.
glassen snow.

SEA BREAM

fierce tough burly bony sea bream.
spiky fins. visored head.
scaly flesh of the fierce streamlined fish.

big red sea bream left on the chopping board untouched for
            a time.
let the knife wait.

winter light collecting on the streamlined fish.
red. vermilion. gold. purple.
diffused reflections.
yellow speckles.
bandit of the Pacific.
eyes forever wide.
glistening.

BRONZE FUJI

after a hundred million years.
oceans of leaves ice-flow carried away.
thunderbirds lost too.

rock thinned.
craggy.

ice clouds.
cross acutest moon.

MINAMI AKITSU*

in rice fields dew drops.
a thousand million suns glistening.
Minami Akitsu.
gorgeous morning for a walk.
Gen (our Kai dog)
Kuro (N's blackie)
Kennedy (O's collie)
Liz (K's crossbred setter)
already used to it raring to get out with me.
two months. only two months I've been here.
Gen! Kuro! not the wheatfield hey!
the rascals at my bidding running wild kicking up dirt and
            light.
by the field bare elms and snowbells.
dangling snake-gourds. and on gourd vermilion morning-
            shine.
(as little like yesterday. as yesterday sky's layout)
each morning differently fresh.
but every freshness classic.
meaning trees and earth.
whistle.
and out of scrub a hundred yards away.
come flying.
first Gen. second Kuro. third Liz. and a poor fourth forlornly
            Kennedy with his bum paw.
(not the fields! not the wheatfields!)

plantain at the rice field's withered edge. speedwell. parsley.
            wild rocambole. dead nettles. and so on.
the beautiful blossoms in winter.
from the start set against summer's heavy greens.
a weight.
wild rocambole and parsley. dead-nettles.
even in December.
flourishing.

* *Minami Akitsu:* the suburb of Tokyo where Kusano makes his home.

where's the weasel.
as yet unseen.

      something weighing at center.
      prickly black ball of devil's-tongue root.
      my stomach.
      sometimes.
      no one knowing of the two bleedings since coming to
          Akitsu.
      but my old friend (terribly old friend) weighs and stays.
      prickly devil's-tongue root.

on the narrow patch through snowbell woods the dogs lined
          up.
for a moment.
then off into pampas grass.
if that's what you want—go.
I'll go myself.
tea fields.
*Dososhin.**
around the farmhouses high *keyaki** and oak and bamboo
          thickets. chestnut and maple too.
roof on roof of leaves.
a shrike shrieks.
at a bend in the path a homemade red mailbox.
in the shopping bag lugged along.
put there by a clerk peanuts eggs toilet paper two cans of
          mackerel.
(feed for the rainbow trout and Gen)
hey! not that way! this!
not to the Nakamura Bakery sign today.
by the Primary School down by the rough slope.

      (something weighing at center!)

fragrance of tea blossoms.
radish and spinach rows.

* *Keyaki:* the common zelkova tree.
  Dososhin: small stone figure—the god of wayfarers—common at road-
    sides.

Dososhin.
and. like a haircurdling cock-crow.
whistle.
all the names at once impossible.
whistle.
four tongues come creeping out of the bushes.
ok let's go home.
same way as day before yesterday now.
hills woods fields and rice fields December.
the sky's beauty also blossoms in winter.

    (oy! the prickly devil's-tongue root weighing at center)

Minami Akitsu.
end of the walk premium.
beyond the thickets.
Fuji.

HALF A SUN

after Fuji's.
left side sun coming in.
from top north.
flowing steep down perhaps no cloud.
quick black snow smoke.
shaking sinking sliding away. moment.
jumps.
crimson pudding.
o half a sun now.
mightiest member of the universe.
blind my two upstanding eyes with a whack of light.

BLUE JINTA*

jagged peaked mountain of rock. in almost equilateral triangle eastward towers. at its base a limitless waste known as the Place of Ashes extends. in the South and North Vietnam War there three hundred years ago but. also through war upon war thereafter the number of human beings was appreciably diminished. so many mixed marriages. pure blacks or pure Japanese rare.

now. in the Place of Ashes a spiral glass tower stands. pennants with "midsummer craziness" flutter atop it. eighteen pieces of felt. rigged in a crescent but. one for the jinta shack. the other seventeen resting places for frogs.

(originally frogs preferred temperate zones. tropical zones. subtropical zones and moisture but. since the 1900s those like the spadefoot toad have burrowed into the desert country around Arizona.) wine-colored twilight came on. the spiral glass tower was lit with arterial red and blue neon and when the "funny circus" of illuminated news ran through the air the frogs swarmed out of their seventeen resting places.

the jinta made up of clarinet cornet bass drum & tambourine
        blares away &.
(the simplest sort without any big fat boss or madman or
        gangling slave.)
the jinta blares away &.
one frog a dead ringer for Marilyn Monroe begins to sing her
        come-on.

---

* *Jinta:* a small raggletail musical troupe and their tinny type of music.

24

new earth steaming.
day and night stewing in hot springs.
lepidodendra fans.
fanning hot flesh.

till earth cools.
scorpions bay at the moon.
black mist in the city.
lung cancer crowing.

(old! old!)
(marvellous! queen bee.)
this is really 20th-century stuff.

suddenly Gambi leaps a good 45 feet. coming
down with a twirl like an ice skater.
—don't need no ladder.
—nor big cellophane net.
nor rope nor even frankly trapeze to perch on
but.
suddenly now a swing for six.
the jinta blaring away &.
all six jostling each other.
floating swinging seaweed cookies.
        yun yun yun yuyuyun
        yun yun yuyuyun
in the air the song starting to flow.

        the Ashura heaven immense.
        look. immense.
        with all that humidity.
        praise the great air!
        look!

everywhere litmus-blue &.
the spiral glass neon in a flash lights more &.
over the top of the peaked mountain a full moon.
(far more pockmarked than in the 20th century.)

all over the wasteland so much diamond dust.
the jinta blaring away &.
in the midst of the Place of Ashes however Himulali.

    in the blazing heart.
    oenothera makiana.
    the moon-colored flower.

    the mirage lake ripples.
    the sad stretch of it.
    in your heart.
    my moon-colored.
    flower float.

(eh——. rice-crackers and caramels.)

—somebody seems to be crazy somewhere.
lemonade and rice-cracker vendors, etc., there aren't any.
(ok. I'll try it the old traditional way.)

    in the heavenly
   brilliance in the breath of
    a perfect spring day
  the quiet heart is undone
  when the cherry blossoms fall.

(don't mock. the feeling's no good.)
(classic. great.)
(mockery's a vice. vice.)

the jinta blaring away &.
in the great space with a hop skip and a jump.
one after another bewilderingly.
the one leaping last a limping beauty.

(hey Lilimu. your asshole's showing.)
(wa! ha! ha!)
(wa! ha! ha!)
(wa! ha! ha!)

26

the jinta blares away &.
the chorus line begins.
like human beings with belly-buttons.
like human beings growing hair.
the chorus making a ring in the Place of Ashes.
viscera waggling transparently.
>ahahahahahah.
>blare away cornet bass drum.
>now all of you.
>like man have fallen.
>rararan rararan rararararan
>rararan rararan rararararan

(hey! cut it out. stop it.)
a deep voice booming.
the "honest march" of electrified news flowing into air.

>our brains are little but.
>our hearts big (we've got plenty of nerve).
>on this side and the other of the earth.
>we're smiling.
>>*marchons marchons marchons*
>we've got no weapons but.
>our lives rise and fall.
>in the hot wastes and gasp but.
>>*marchons marchons marchons*
>beget. flourish. go on. go on.

in scrimmages (fractions of diamond dust).
thousands of frogs surge forth.
the jinta shrieks and reaches climax.
in air.
snake fireworks begin to run.
ten thousand firework snakes.
shooshoopoon shooshooshoosh confusion.
from the top of the peaked mountain.
booo-wham big cascading fireworks.
casting out nets.

shrieking jinta.
smoking full moon.
on earth great waves of frogs waves.

HACHIJO* RHAPSODY

       dadadan dadadan dadadan dadadan dan dan
       dan dan dan dan dah dah dah

night wind licking the Kurashio crawls over the field &.
three bonfires blaze.
cra-ra-rackling.
swinging flames.
       dan dan dan dan
boys leopardskins round their waists.
drumsticks carving the wind &.
       dan dan dadadan
(dancing dance barebreasted crescent moon clinging there.)
August's great festival of life.
dance. drink. devour. drink. devour. dance.
a giant tossing rotten dry mackerel into his gaping gullet.
(and tagobe* too. taro. and so much bamboo-shoot potato.)
from a Jomon* cup demon-killing liquor.
big women drinking up brims of rice-brandy. (hot mist
burning belly) young female deer. imps snivelling.
let yourself go old women! topaz women.
dance dance.

       wheel of the sun ah-doro ah-doro ah-doro
       wheel of the moon ginga ginga ginga.
       praised be heaven and earth!
       o Gods. sing.

lice in wild stringy hair clinging to the shaking in crawling
       into pores &.
crescent jade necklace swinging at breasts yun yun pulling
       torn off.

       dan dan dan dan dan dan dan kakaka dan
       kakaka dan kakakakakah dan kakakat dan dan kat
       dan ka dan dan dan dan dan dan dan dan dan kakakat

* Hachijo: island in Tokyo Bay formerly place of exile.
  Tagobe: local country food.
  Jomon: ancient rope-pattern pottery of unglazed clay.

oh. praise fire.
praise wind.
praise water.
praise earth.
praise sea-turtle and wild grass.
praise the life in all that lives.
praise cunnus and phallus.

    dan dan dadadan

Brahms' satellite rising.
from the dead end of heaven's line.
along the shores of the Milky Way.
through the center of the Swan's belly and lost in the depths
       of heaven.
oh. the long past and the long future commingle and make
       what is new strong. da da da.
yesterday and today languishing here and there make what is
       new weak. da da da.
bonfires blazing crackle.

(pasania-wood. camphorwood burn anything.)
       dan dan dan dan
Hachijo night unadvancing.
Brahms' satellite!
*Kojiki** friend!

    dan dan dan dan dadadan dadadan
    dah dah dah dah dadadan dah dada

* *Kojiki:* Japanese legendary.

30

UNTITLED

Fuji.
in the West set.

        a full moon.

in the East floats.
lifts.

MONOLOGUE OF A HIBERNATING FROG

sleet   or snow?
feels good it soaks into.
my body wet.
mistily moistened.
snow   or cold rain?
acanthus rooting above me gone bad for the cold?
or those withered leaves suffering heavy snow?
what's that faint sound coming on?
a jet?
or a big truck?
like electric massage feels good.
never get hungry.
underground this may be hell.
I think hell is fine.
the dreams I dream always wrapped in a rose mist.
meanwhile spring arrives and. cool-like.
into the dazzling light and air I creep up but.
that's what makes me smile with all my eyes.

RECOVERY

blessed is recovery.
bounce of happiness.
the healthy always screwing themselves up.
such joy beyond their savoring.

for crumbs.
unknown to the doctor.
pigeons every day come to the terrace.
this morning first time as many as nine and.
finally come down to this room.

out the window leaden.
clouds everywhere making a great wall but.
beyond it.
to the ultramarine heaven.
wanting to say "good morning."
that's how I feel.

CANAPÉS

split cracker in my teeth.
butter a bit. upon it.
set *miso*-pickled *shiso* seeds and crunch it.
on another bit spread home-made huckleberry jam.
on another piece blue cheese.
on butter of another pickled-plum juice.
on another buttered but winterblossoms from the rose
            garden.
for the rye bread Cid Corman's wife made for me.
on its thin slices blue cheese.
on Camembert a drop of rolled in *shiso* pickled-apricot juice.
now some British gooseberry preserve.
now some salmon roe on butter.
now some fermented soybeans with powdered yolk.
like a funny mixed-up way of EastWest playing house.

THE MOON

walking I was.
trampling fallen leaves.

moon rose.

and I.
turned into the street.

and again.
turn into a path.

BITING

—childhood nostalgia—

the Abukuma range was gentle-sloping.

and I.
often gnawed at.
pencil and.
lead.

Abukuma's heaven blue.
clouds flowed slowly on.

but I.
often gnawed at.
the edge of my wrinkled Japanese reader and.
when I gnawed into the text.
I had to remember the lost parts.

the primary school stood alone in the rice fields.
in the shimmering spring haze.

but I bit a girl on the arm and.
was severely reprimanded by the teacher.

quiet *susuki*-grass* hill and.
the days' *uguisu*.*

but I.
in a rage had a fit.
with a bucket of water dashed over me.
finally came to.

* *susuki* is pampas grass.
  the *uguisu* (harbinger of spring) is the bush warbler, sometimes wrongly
    called the nightingale; a foothill tiny bird—very shy—and with a lovely
    characteristic sequence of notes.

I never cut my fingernails.
instead of scissors.
used my teeth.

at one spot in the gentle-sloping Abukuma hills.
it was sheer high granite.
holding onto an iron chain I climbed but.

the ruggedness of that Mt. Futatsuya.
was what I was in childhood.

Abukuma's heaven blue.
clouds flowed slowly on though.

I EAT

I eat.
raw beef.
raw horse meat.
raw chicken meat.

I can if I try but don't eat.
pork cutlets.
fried chicken.
prawn tempura.

I eat.
raw (cut and cleaned) prawn.
I don't eat.
lobster with mayonnaise.

I smack my lips over.
darkgreen ear-shell guts.
raw freshwater crabs.

I drink.
snake-liver *sake* brewed in Goshu.
I sip.
snap-turtle blood.

when I was catching char at Teijirozawa in Oku-nikko.
I swallowed a Nikko salamander I happened to find in
looking for worms amongst the rocks.
but such a queer-looking job.
I'll never eat again.

I don't eat.
things made tasteless though tasty themselves.

I eat.
snakes tigers whatever tastes good.

pity us—Buddha.
(money's a consideration though.)

CERTAIN DAYS

1.
wearing a summer hat.
walked out into powdery snow.

looked over a temporary store of radish put up
        for the Abukuma Folk Art Museum. inspected
        and selected those transferred to the
        library yard after being rolled.

scooping up carp and rainbow trout with a landing net.
loosed them into the pool of the 13th night.

snowing in sunlight.

2.
woke at 4:30 a.m.
searched the cupboard.
drank homebrew *sake*.
sucked a ripe persimmon.

3.
walking along the frosty ranks reviewing the garden trees in
        winter decay.
basking in the newborn sunlight a 67-year-old man on his
        way.
to bread, *natto** and work gloves.

walking.
half the sky pale ultramarine.
the other gutter rat gray clouds.
upper half of the hills brimming sunshine.
in summer machine-stitched pants.
the 67-year-old wearing sleeveless *kimono* over a black
        sweater.

* *natto* is a rather viscid bean dressing usually for rice.

in a bag some extra.
mochi,* slices of seaweed, carrots, etc.

back home.
rainbow icicles hanging from the waterpipe.
the 67-year-old chewing and swallowing them.

4.
ground a T'ang ink stick.*
wrote words.
drew bamboo.
and read a book.
ate fish and greens.
perfect.

5.
a young bicycle-racer friend.
      (attempted suicide-violence-bloodletting.)
out of his head report of it came.

6.
light powdery snow.
dancing in wind.
sank in the pool.

(life and death together in my inmost.)
(flickering.)

Tenzan Library.*
mats perched on.

---

* *mochi* is a cake of rice dough: a staple in Japan.
  T'ang ink stick would be a very old stick of Chinese *sumi* ink and much
    prized.
  The Tenzan Library is the Kusano library in the native mountains of the
    poet west of Tokyo—created by his friends.

MOURNING/MISUNDERSTANDING

1.
Shimpei-san. may you live long.

received from you.
this your last word.

Nakagiri.*
sooner or later I'll also be on the way to the third homeland.
said to be so dark likely hard to recognize each other in
                    passing.

no more.
and no more chance to meet.

    you were drunk at the festival here lost your shoes and.
    went back to Tokyo in slippers.

(surviving only in memory.)

2.
a call from my house saying publisher C's Mr. S confirmed he
was alive in a hospital in Ome.

wept.

* Nakagiri is Kusano's poet-friend Nakagiri Masao.

INCIDENTALLY

38.9° C.
new Tokyo heat record.

and at the other end of the earth.
very slowly.
an ice floe the size of Shikoku* is on the move.

* Shikoku is the smallest of the Japanese main islands.

SNOW

"on the rocks" a mistake.
into a glass of Old Parr snow sunk.
drink.

(snow falling thick.)

heaven indeed.
extravagance be praised.

looking at me.
Leo's* lapis eyes.
an instant.
like a blue universe.

drink.

* Leo is Kusano-san's Siamese cat.

SNOW *SAKE*

in the afternoon.
against the rules.
drinking "one cup" of cold *sake*.
out the window.
snow drifting down.
all around.
no murder.
no sound of mah jongg tiles.
the sound of no sound drifting down and.
even my pulse beyond hearing.
alone in Jōmon* times yet.
again down my throat it flows.

* The Jōmon (rope-pattern pottery) age refers to prehistoric Japan.

THE EEL "U-KICHI"*

"U-kichi" the eel.
lifts his face from the pond.
takes food from between my fingers.
flickeringly leisurely.
heads back to the deep end.

       "U-kichi" the eel.
       putting food in the feeder.
       my shape.
       from the pond saw.

"U-kichi" the eel.
again returns.
lifts his face from the pond.
takes food from between my fingers.
flickeringly leisurely.
heads back to the deep end.

* The name "U-kichi" is: "U" (eel) plus the male diminutive—colloquial affection.

FOSSIL FISH

about a billion years B.C. fossil fish.
now.
stretched out before me.
Brazil's Xingu riverside sedimentary deposit hardened.

length 28 cm.
width 6 cm.
tiny scales perfectly aligned tail taut.

a fish makes no name for itself.

this no name 28 cm. swam at ease. another time.
flashed on the face of the waters leaping sometimes perhaps.

    between the fossil and me.
now.
time past.

    between the fossil and me.
    now.
    time past.

a fish become stone.
a billion years ago Xingu's waters.
was it nice then?

become stone no name fish.
scales perfectly your body.
from Brazil put on a boat crossed the Pacific you now.
Japan, Tokyo, Higashimurayama, Akitsu-goko in the Kusano
        house mute.

    between the fossil fish and me.
now.
    time passes.
    clouds passing.

soon I too will have turned into mere bone.
no name you are neat.
this is as it is forever and ever perhaps.

FROG SWALLOWING A FIREFLY

a frog a firefly.
gulped down.

face aglow.
face lit up from within body.
little circular blue gaslight.

then turned off.

in the sky a crescent moon.

color unclear though.
without glitter.
gleaming.

POTATOES

late at night secretly.
drinking some potent Chinese wine.
eight potatoes.

washed in water.
skins on.
eight raw potatoes.

standing there alone in the kitchen.
for the first time became.
wine appetizers.

not cooked crumbly soft.
but a strange clear color.
on the crunchy side.

POTATO & ONION CONVERSATION

P: Not exactly round. but we're pretty close to it.
O: optimistic you. just get into a kitchen and you've had it.
P: people eat us. that's our life.
O: you think so. that's never been my sense of it.
P: stay in the ground and you flower.
O: still—to be eaten *is* life. I want to be enjoyed eaten.
P: in that case you have to understand the taste of texture.
O: yes. you and I are utterly different. a slice of me
            pungent.
P: still. people ate us raw. that was a new experience—eh.
            surprised. that was Shimpei Kusano.
O: ha. only small talk. anyway you get the best sense of a
            thing fresh. thinking leads to cooking.
P: so you're a fatalist.
O: humans also die. in the ground is staying alive.
P: if alive is dead. ha.

CUCKOO

(cuckoo singing.)
((ah. ah. singing. singing.))
(come 'ere.)
speaking.
I close the book go out stand on the porch.
(isn't singing?)
((not hearing.))
I come back to get a hearing aid.
ah—there's S. bringing it.
abandoning myself sitting crosslegged.

cuckoo.
cuckoo.
some ten years ago by the Yanasegawa in a thicket cuckoo
          song.
growing within me.
not head not ear not memory somewhere unknown vividly
          cuckoo doing its thing.
some ten years end of historic time.
within me being restored.

CHANCE

can't sleep turn on the light.
by the pillow the electric clock.
four four four.*

me.
death death death the association.

(one long long minute.)

little by little I.

*hsi hsi hsi.**
have denied it.

now smoke a cigarette.
the smoke winding up.

---

* In Japanese the number 4 and the word for death (*shi*) are homonyms.
  Kusano-san uses the Chinese word *hsi* (pronounced *ki* in Japanese): which
    means "Happy New Year."

ASKING MYSELF/ANSWERING MYSELF

un un. un un.
un un.

mm mm. mm mm.
mm.

ah ah. ah ah.
ah.

(shut up.)

(can't say a word.)

BIRTHDAY

in the history of the world.
not even .000000000001 mm.
my history.

but night and day have breathed air.
27,740 days.
this is the end.
76.

a single eye.

sharp ear.

somewhere.
spring thunder's.
presentiment.

UNDERGROUND TALK

o dear. rain.
don't be silly. it's snow.
but it isn't white.
where do you think we are?
underground.
and the snow melting filters through. the weight is different.

then. midwinter's coming?
now. you've got it.
a long way yet to spring.
becoming a year older underground.
I don't like it. becoming an old woman.
is that what I look like?
Qayloqay said. she had rare incomparable heavenly eyes.
in spring I trust to have sight. those heavenly mentioned eye
          things. it's very dark here you know.